P9-DXH-673

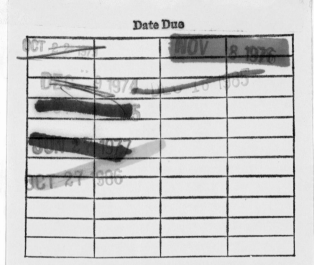

TREES OF THE WEST

"To find new things,
   the path to take today
   is the path you took yesterday."

JOHN BURROUGHS

Other Books by Matilda Rogers

TREES
OF THE WEST
IDENTIFIED AT A GLANCE

BY MATILDA ROGERS
PHOTOGRAPHS BY WYNN HAMMER
FOREWORD BY DR. MILDRED E. MATHIAS

The Ward Ritchie Press

FOREWORD

In this book, Matilda Rogers introduces the common cultivated trees any traveler will see in subtropical areas of the world.

The late George T. Hastings, author of *Trees of Santa Monica*, months before his death, wrote the following original foreword for this book:

Too many people see trees without appreciation of their attractiveness and do not know the names of any of them. They are merely "trees" to them.

In 1951, Matilda Rogers wrote *A First Book of Tree Identification* of eastern trees. The book became popular at once and has remained so. Now she has done the same for some western trees.

The beautiful photographs stress the particular features of each tree which most help to distinguish it. And her concise, non-technical descriptions make it easy for anyone, young or old, not only to recognize and name some forty of the more commonly seen trees but to learn something special about each.

The names given are the "common" names, the ones ordinarily used and of most importance to most people. In addition, she tells of the oldest, tallest, and most massive trees of the world, all western. A list of state trees and several other features add interest.

This book makes a good beginning introduction to trees known to too many only by sight.

Being acquainted with trees is an exciting and satisfying experience. This book is designed to stimulate an interest in identifying trees.

DR. MILDRED E. MATHIAS
Professor of Botany
University of California, Los Angeles

CONTENTS

COLOR SUPPLEMENT

In addition to the black and white photographs, which accompany the text throughout, the following color plates of flowering trees will be found on Pages:

INTRODUCTION

These western trees are introduced as though you were taking a "tree walk" with me, via the camera's lens.

There are over 1,000 kinds of trees in western United States and Canada. Some, of course, are native species; others, hybrids; a great number are cultivated trees, from many foreign countries.

Since there are endless varieties of these trees—several hundreds of the Acacias and Eucalypts alone—this book contains only those shade and ornamental trees most frequently seen while walking or motoring.

The photographs show only the most important identifying characteristics of each tree, whether it be the size or shape, the bark, the leaf, or the flower.

Every tree begins its life in a flower, which produces fruit and seeds. Each tree has its own peculiar type of fruit which contains the seed. Some needle-leaf trees have berries; some bear their seeds in cones. The seeds produce new plants which start the cycle all over again.

Often different names are used for the same tree in different places. Often too, the real or botanical names, in Latin, are long and unpronounceable. In any event, one forgets them easily. I do! I use only a few scientific names—those most commonly known and easiest to remember.

On my recent trip around the world, I saw many of these "Western" trees in different countries. Since scientists ship seeds to all parts of the globe, foreign trees are widely cultivated and, climate permitting, become naturalized almost anywhere.

Many western trees do not lose all their leaves at the same time, as most eastern trees do. They remain green all year round. As some leaves die, new ones appear.

My acquaintance with western trees dates back to 1926-1930 and 1938-1940 when I first lived in the West. For the past three

9

years, I have truly enjoyed studying these trees intensively again. When you are interested in trees, you discover seasonal changes in buds, leaves, flowers, fruit, seeds, and even barks.

On exploring walks, you, too, will have many surprising things crop up, which you may never have noticed before. They may not have been there the week before, when you last saw that particular tree in the very same spot.

Each photograph is accompanied by brief descriptions in non-technical language. Experts will notice that the trees are purposely not arranged botanically but by "look-alikes." This, I hope, will help youngsters, especially, to remember trees more readily.

Because trees are friends and give a lifetime of real pleasure, tree identification is a popular hobby. I can think of no better hobby—casual or serious—for young or old. It adds zest to living. It keeps one outdoors; it costs nothing. Best of all, it creates a fascinating game of absorbing adventure every time one takes a stroll alone or in groups. Always one can find something that is new or different.

At the risk of over-simplifying the problem of identification, I call attention to differences as well as similarities of trees, stressing the chief distinguishing features.

Just as in *A First Book of Tree Identification* of eastern trees, the illustrations and text for each tree here are together. This is important. Nothing confuses or bothers me more than to read about a tree (or anything for that matter) with a photograph of something entirely different on that page—and a footnote reading: "See Fig. No. so-and-so, Page so-and-so" for the one I am reading about!

No matter where you live or travel, I hope this practical book will enable you to greet each of these trees by name wherever you may see any. Once you know them, you can have the added pleasure of introducing these trees to your friends.

MATILDA ROGERS
Santa Monica, California

TREES OF THE WEST
Identified at a Glance

MEXICAN FAN PALMS

Almost the first thing that impresses a newcomer to the southern part of the West is that avenues and highways are lined with different species of Palm trees of different heights.

These Palms are an ornamental feature of the landscape. They add an exotic touch. While Palms belong to tropical parts of the world, there are millions of them here in the West.

The tallest of these trees are called Mexican Fan Palms. Some are about a hundred feet high and a hundred years old.

Palms do not have branches or twigs—just leaves and trunks. As new leaves develop, the tree grows older and taller.

Of all the Palms, the Mexican Fan has the slimmest trunk. You will notice that each appears "swollen" at the base, then tapers a bit, and the rest of the cylindrical trunk is straight, tall, and slender.

Mexican Fan trees often have a basket-weave pattern on part of the lower third of the trunk. This criss-cross latticework design is from the remains of old leaves—actually the leftovers of the stiff base fibres of previous leaf stalks. The bark is a dull gray.

Dead leaves, hugging the top of the trunk, resemble fringed hula skirts. A good strong wind tears them loose, or tree trimmers saw them off (with their sky-high hydraulic boom and saw machinery).

Since the leaves of a Mexican Fan Palm are so high up, all you can see is that they form a sort of circle at the top, that each leaf is slashed, and that each has a long stalk. Only when you see a dead leaf on the ground can you tell that it is about three feet long and has an equally long stalk, and that the stalk has sharp spikes on both edges.

In late September or early October, if you are lucky enough to pass by when the tree trimmers are on the job, you can get a close-up of still another kind of stalk. It is long, tan, and spikeless. On each of these spikeless stalks there are about six dangling, corn-like tassels. Each of these tassels, in turn, is a cluster of numerous, lovely white flowers.

FAN PALMS

When you pass a seedling, you can really get a close-up of the Fan Palm. It is interesting to watch fan-shaped leaves develop. When a new Palm leaf shoots up, through the center of a group of leaves, it is closed, thin, and upright. It looks like a bright green sword. It opens slowly and gradually.

When the new leaf is fully opened, it begins to lean outward toward the other fan leaves. Next, some of the older ones begin to droop backwards. Later, the very oldest and lowest leaves become yellow and dry, just before turning brown. That is when they hang and hug the tree.

Each fan-shaped leaf is roundish. The leaves of all Fan Palms are about as wide as they are long. California Fan leaves grow to six feet; the Mexican Fan to three feet; and the Windmill Fan only eighteen inches to two feet. Each leaf stalk grows in length to almost the size of the leaf.

Each stalk starts out rather narrow but by the time a leaf has matured, it may—on a six foot leaf—reach six inches wide.

Most fan leaf stalks have sharp saw-like spikes on both edges. They prick. A mere touch and your finger bleeds!

Fan Palm leaves are "pleated." They are solid only on the lower half. The upper half is slit into many folded, ribbon-like strips.

Orioles like to weave their nests into the creases of these fan-shaped leaves. You should see what strong and artistic knots the orioles tie with the threads on a leaf!

Each green leaf has long, twisting, fine, thread-like fibres. These hang loosely from the tips and sides of each division and form an interesting spiderweb design across the leaf.

If you will look closely at the lower right of the photograph, you will also see a couple of stalks of other leaves underneath this one. Note how sturdy the spikes are, even on a seedling.

There are many species of Fan Palms. All are evergreen. The quickest way to identify the three most common Palms, with fan-shaped foliage such as this, is to remember that:

THE MEXICAN FAN PALM *has the slimmest trunk and is the tallest tree.*

THE CALIFORNIA FAN PALM *is much shorter and has the stoutest trunk.*

THE WINDMILL FAN PALM, *the shortest of these three, has a tapered trunk completely covered with a dark, gauze-like substance.*

The California Fan is our only native Palm. It is also known as *Washingtonia filifera*, in honor of George Washington. Originally a desert tree, it seems to thrive in canyons and on city streets. Many an avenue is lined with them.

Only the young tree trunks are covered with the stiff stalk remnants of former leaves in a basket-weave design. All older trees have smooth, stout, sturdy, elephant-gray trunks, as shown by the tops of the two trees in our photograph.

These massive, unbranched, erect trunks resemble concrete building colums. They are about two and a half feet in diameter, and may reach straight up to a height of fifty to seventy feet.

CALIFORNIA FAN PALM

The round leaves of the California Fan, or Washingtonia, are the largest of all fan palms. Some reach to six feet in length. They are as wide as they are long and have stalks as long or longer.

Most California Fan trees may have as many as forty or more large, pale green, fan-shaped leaves around the crown. The newer the foliage, the more upright the leaf.

The other leaves spread out at varying angles, exposing the long, wide, leaf stalks. Their sharp thorns, on both edges, may be visible if the stalk is silhouetted against the sky or if the tree is short enough.

Since California Fan trees are shorter than the Mexican Fan, spikeless stalks with the corn-tassels of flowers are also visible in October. Being tan, they stand out among the green leaves.

The edges of all leaves are slashed half way down, having been frayed by wind. You cannot see that the lower part of the leaves are "pleated," nor can you see the thread-like fibre, except on low, young seedlings.

But you can see dead leaves hanging loosely near the very top of the trunk. Dead California Fan leaves hang on longer than any other. Since their stalks are the longest and strongest of all fan palms, the wind is not apt to tear them off. To be removed, each leaf stalk requires sawing.

All too many Washingtonia Fan trees are neglected, especially on private property. Often there are as many as a dozen rows of fringed hula skirt tunics, reaching half way down the tree.

Since the thatch-like masses are a real fire hazard, many cities employ tree trimmers to remove these dead leaves periodically.

WINDMILL FAN PALMS

Windmill Fan Palms, very small trees imported originally from China, are common everywhere.

In California, Windmill Fan Palms adorn many front lawns. On streets, they are often planted in groups of three or more.

Because of its shape and odd trunk, it is the easiest Palm to recognize. It has no bark at all.

From top to bottom, the trunk is completely covered with a coarse, dark, brown or charcoal-gray, hairy substance.

The Windmill Fan Palm is a most peculiar-looking tree, not only because of its tangled gauze-like trunk but because the tree itself tapers so the trunk is narrowest at the bottom!

The Windmill Palm is the shortest of the three most common types of fan palms. It has the smallest sized leaves.

The round fan-shaped leaves are as wide as they are long—only eighteen inches to two feet—with stalks the same length. The stalks are the shortest as well as the narrowest of the fan palms. They have spikes.

As with all palms, Windmill Fan leaves grow all around at the top of the tree.

If you will look closely at our photograph, you will see between the top two center leaves a profusion of flowers in drooping sprays. These golden-yellow flowers on slender stalks are conspicuous, since they cascade among the green leaves. Later, chartreuse-yellow pea-sized fruit appear on these long thin stems.

Our photograph also gives you a close-up of several layers of hula skirts, hugging the trunk on all sides. Since Windmill Fan leaves are small, these few tiers do not look as unkempt as the larger and longer layers of dead leaves on Mexican or California Fan Palms.

Another kind of Palm, of which there are also many species, is the Feather Palm with its long leaves, divided feather-fashion.

Feather Palms are alike only in that the swaying fronds have a strong midrib with many folded divisions on both sides. The long fronds themselves taper to a point.

The three most common Feather Palms are:

THE QUEEN, *which has the most graceful and plume-like leaves*
THE KING, *which has heavier and less flexible fronds and*
THE CANARY ISLAND DATE, *which has the stiffest leaves.*

QUEEN PALM

The Queen Palm, a favorite, familiarly known as Cocos plumosa (a name no longer used by botanists), is a fairly tall, slim tree. It decorates many a private lawn, patio, and city parkway in warm areas. It is a popular street tree and lends a romantic touch to any landscape.

The Cocos plumosa has few leaves. Some trees have only six fronds; others, as many as twenty. They are bright green. The dangling fronds droop gracefully and sway with the breeze.

The Queen's leaf is so soft, flexible, and graceful that it is actually more of a plume than a feather. Because it has more leaflets at the midrib, its foliage is denser than most palms of the feather type.

Each soft blade-like leaflet is folded at the midrib, then opens fully and comes to a point at the tip. The plume-like fronds, which are often fifteen feet long and three to four feet wide, taper to a point.

These enormous leaves form a handsome spray at the top of the tree.

The bark of the Queen is light gray. It looks smooth, but if you touch it, you will find it has a surface like cement—not only in color but also in hardness.

As the photograph shows, the most distinguishing feature of any Queen Palm is the large bulging bract, immediately below the lowest leaf. This bract, at least two feet high, gives the appearance of a bulb split into three-pointed prongs. It is this leaf base by which you can most easily recognize a Queen Palm anywhere.

In October, just below some leaves, you will notice large flower clusters with numerous tiny flowers cascading out of brown spathes. Some flowers are cream-colored; some, chartreuse. On other trees, the thin stalks will already be covered with green fruit. At first, these are pea-sized; by June, the fruit will have reached grape-size.

The striking King Palm is known under many names; *Seaforthia elegans*, for one. Some call it *Loroma amethystina*. There are still three other "preferred" Latin names—each of which is long enough to take up a whole line.

This ornamental tree comes originally from Australia. It is popular, but is not seen on as many boulevards as the graceful Queen Palm.

Our photograph gives you at least three valuable distinguishing characteristics, described on the opposite page. Once you know these, you will never confuse a King Palm with any Queen—as so many persons do.

KING PALM

First of all, notice that the stately King Palm has a slim, smooth, upward-tapering, tight, green sheath, immediately below the lowest leaf at the top.

Next, the flowers, instead of being directly under the leaves on top, are about three feet below, at the bottom of the sheath.

Each of these flower or fruit clusters has numerous string-like spikes hanging in fountain-like sprays. Each spray is covered with a great number of tiny, beautiful, amethyst-colored flowers. When the flowers have turned to fruit, they look like strings of bright red beads.

The leaf is not as flexible or graceful as the Queen frond. The King has a spray of stiff fronds, about ten or more feet long and three or more feet wide. Each feathery leaf has numerous divisions. The longest of these is eighteen inches long and two inches wide. Each division, like the frond itself, tapers to a point.

Our photograph also shows the habit of growth of new leaves of all Palm trees; they shoot straight up in the center and look like a sword.

The King Palm has a smooth, slender trunk. Like the Queen, the King also has dark, black, ring scars around the trunk from top to bottom, where former leaves had grown.

The bark is cement-like only in color. Here the similarity with the Queen Palm ends.

To my surprise, the day we took this photograph, Wynn Hammer's young son, Loren, accidentally touched the bark with his fingernail. He shouted: "Look, water comes out!"

The King bark is so exceedingly soft, it oozes at the merest touch —and a blackish mark is left.

Not for nothing is this tree known as Seaforthia!

CANARY ISLAND DATE PALM

Canary Island Date Palms are tall, stately, stout trees with huge sprays of gigantic feather-like leaves. They are popular ornamental street trees everywhere.

Each tree has fifty to one hundred of these long, glossy, hardy leaves. The fronds are dark, bluish-green, ten to twenty feet long and two or more feet wide. They are tight and stiff—actually the stiffest of the three popular feather palms.

Feather palm leaves do not have stalks; they do have a strong midrib. When the tree is silhouetted against the sky, you again notice the spaces created by the wedge-shaped leaflets, at both sides of the midrib.

Each frond tapers to a point, and each division, while pointed at its tip, is over an inch wide at the midrib, where it is folded in half and then opens up.

As with all Palms, the newer leaves at the crown are the most upright. The mature fronds arch outward in layers, fountain-like. As early as August, the oldest and lowest of the numerous leaves begin to wilt at the edges and then turn brown. At this point, they begin to droop and are finally blown off by gusty winds or have to be sawed off.

In August, September and October, in among the glossy green leaves, the bright orange color of the seed stems attracts attention.

On some trees, huge flower clusters cascade out of woody, boat-shaped spathes, at the base of the leaves. On a male tree the tiny flowers are cream-colored. On a female tree they are greenish-white. The flowers droop in enormous bunches on long, thin, branching spikes.

The blossoms on the female trees are followed later by orange-colored fruit which hangs loosely on these drooping, wavy spikes.

These "dates" are about the size of small olives but are not edible.

Canary Island Date Palm seedlings look like huge pineapples. Mature trees are trimmed so that the pineapple design remains at the top of the thick trunk, directly under the feather-duster effect of the foliage.

The rest of the rough bark, on the enormous trunks of these conspicuous trees, is covered with semi-circular scarmarks. These create an interesting all-over design, showing where each leaf had been.

The base of each Canary Island Date Palm is swollen, sometimes to a diameter of about five or six feet. The trunk then tapers quickly into a two-and-a-half foot width and shoots straight up fifty to seventy feet or more.

25

YUCCA

When most people hear the name Yucca, they think of the native California plant which grows on hillsides and is known as "The Candle of the Lord."

Another well-known and popular Yucca species is the desert Joshua Tree.

There are many species of Yucca, originally imported from the West Indies and elsewhere. Several species are natives of Arizona, New Mexico, and California.

Yucca trees, like palms (which they are often called by mistake), have no branches or twigs. In addition to trunks and leaves, they have conspicuous spiky clusters of flowers.

Although our photograph was taken early in August, the tree had only four upright clusters of the large bell-shaped waxy flowers. You can spot them at the very top. The flowers are creamy-white and fragrant. Most Yucca plants flower earlier in the summer.

Six weeks later, when I passed this same tree again, four other flower clusters were out in full bloom. Meantime, the ones shown here, as well as many which had blossomed since, had already gone to seed.

This particular tree has several trunks originating from its base. It almost looks like a clump of trees.

The bark of these multiple trunks is gray, scaly, and deeply fissured. The wood is fibrous.

Yucca is usually found only in the desert, but as you will see from our photograph, this particular tree flourishes right in a civic center.

Even a casual traveler could not fail to notice it.

THE EUCALYPTS

The first Eucalyptus or Gum tree planted in San Francisco was imported from Australia over a hundred years ago. Today, there are millions of these evergreen trees throughout the western part of the United States.

In the southern part of California and Arizona, you see rows of Eucalypts alternating with Palms. They are used as ornamental trees, especially on boulevards, in parks, and in gardens.

Miles of Eucalypts are also planted as windbreaks. In southern California, they protect the citrus groves. Further north, they border sugar-beet fields, cotton fields, and other crops.

One of the striking characteristics of the majestic Gum tree is that there are different kinds of leaves on different parts of the same tree. These differ in shape, size, color, and texture.

For instance, juvenile leaves come out, in pairs, on squarish stems. The leaves are short, wide, blue-gray, and sessile (that is, they have no individual stalks).

Transitional leaves are also blue-gray but they are longer and narrower.

Adult leaves are very long and narrow. They hang loosely, alternately, and obliquely on individual stalks, one to two inches long.

The edges are smooth on all leaves. Most of the leaves are lopsided at the base of the midvein. Some adult leaves are curved; others, sickle-shaped. Some grow to twelve inches long and two and a half inches wide. They are dark green, thick, and leathery.

In the fall, many of these leaves change to a lovely maroon color before they fall off. At almost any season, some trees shed a few leaves.

Eucalyptus seedpods vary greatly also. On some trees, they are smooth; on some, wrinkled; still others are ribbed, and some have cups or bowls or woody buttons.

This Blue Gum leaf is the leaf you will see most, since it is said that eighty percent of all Eucalypts, in the United States as well as in their native Australia, are Blue Gum trees. They predominate the landscape everywhere in the West.

Most Eucalyptus trees exude a gummy substance, which accounts for the "Gum" in the name. The flowers, stems, barks, buds, and fruit, as well as the leaves, contain an aromatic oil.

Eucalypts have a medicinal fragrance, especially after it rains.

Experts say there are over 600 different species. Some fare best in cold areas, others in warm and moist places. In their native land, they grow as high as 300 feet. Here in the United States, some grow over 100 feet.

As you see from the photograph below, long, vigorous new shoots sometimes grow out horizontally near the bottom of huge trunks of Blue Gum trees.

Extremely tall Eucalyptus trees often have divided trunks.

Since the true bark sheds in strips during summer or early fall, the massive trunk has a blotchy appearance.

Note the handsome trunk of this tree with its many pastel colors, including plum, tan, pink, blue, and white.

The above close-up of a new shoot shows that the juvenile twigs are four-angled; that is, the stems are square instead of round.

Note, too, that these Blue Gum juvenile leaves grow directly on the twig, in pairs, without individual leaf stalks. The leaves have a waxy surface and are much shorter and broader than the adult leaves. They are blue-gray.

Notice also the two clusters of flower buds. *Eucalyptus* means well-covered. Each flower bud is covered by a cap. When it is ready to bloom, the cap blows off. On some trees, the caps are flat, on some rounded, on still others, long and pointed.

These long, narrow, adult lance-shaped leaves and bell-like fruit are Blue Gum. These leaves turn a lovely maroon and feel leathery.

Each leaf has an individual stalk; the main stem is no longer square.

Note too that the blue-gray fruit has raised ridges and that each grows singly.

Eucalyptus leaves and fruit contain an oil which gives them a characteristic odor.

Some Blue Gum trees blossom in November, others in the spring. Then the blue-gray buds burst open and the caps fall to the ground.

The flowers are clusters of numerous fine, silk threads, radiating from a center, in a one-and-a-half inch circle. The flowers are white on most trees; on some, cream-colored.

The adult outer brown bark of this Eucalyptus tree peels off in strips and often hangs in long ribbons until it falls off.

Note the smooth inner bark showing through the bark on both sides.

Strips as long as twenty feet, from one to five inches wide, have been seen on some Eucalyptus trees.

In Australia, they also call some of the Eucalypts "Stringy-bark."

Thanks to florist shops, which sell these leaves everywhere, millions of men and women know this as Eucalyptus, even though they may never have seen a live Eucalyptus tree.

It is familiarly known as the Silver Dollar Eucalyptus. It looks as though the stem grew right through the center of each leaf. Actually, two separate leaves grow opposite each other; neither has an individual stalk. This foilage is silvery or gray-green and has a pungent odor.

The Silver Dollar Eucalyptus is very decorative in flower arrangements. It blends beautifully with live pink or white carnations. It will keep for months without water.

The divided trunks of this towering Weeping Eucalyptus tree are massive. The tree gets its name from the drooping branches, as much as from its foliage. It is also known as Red Gum.

The whitish trunks, though smooth, have mottled blotches, somewhat like Sycamore trees.

Each of the trunks of this tree has a large number of drooping branches, which, in turn, have many drooping twigs. Each twig has a considerable number of short, slender, willow-like leaves.

35

RED IRON-BARK

Still another Eucalyptus with willow-like leaves is the Red Iron-bark.

The leaves are slender, four to six inches long. The long stems and branches droop.

Note how different this bark is from most Eucalyptus trees. It is black, rough, and furrowed.

The trunk and bark look more like an oak than a Eucalyptus.

The Red Iron-bark is a medium-sized tree. It flowers in June and again in December. The flowers are pink.

LEMON-SCENTED EUCALYPTUS

This tall, graceful, ornamental tree requires a warm climate. The lemon-scented trees are also called *Citriodora*. They are often planted in groups of three.

The leaves on these trees were so high up that our photograph shows the shaggy bark of one tree while the leaves belong to two of its neighbors.

Some of these lofty, spindly trees get to be 130-foot giants.

Lemon-scented Eucalyptus leaves are narrow and pointed, only five inches long and three quarters of an inch wide. Each has its own short stalk. When crushed, the leaves have a distinct fragrance of lemon.

In September and October, the street is littered with beautiful, red or brownish leaves; yet the leaves on the tree remain bright green.

After the thin, loose outer bark peels off, the slender trunks remain smooth. Some are yellow-white; others are flesh-colored.

A common street tree which decorates long avenues everywhere is the Red or Scarlet Flowering Eucalyptus. It has a rough, furrowed bark, which, like the Red Iron-bark, does not peel.

The leaves of the Flowering Eucalyptus are short, three to five inches long and almost half as wide. They are dark green, thin, and soft. They turn bronze in August.

Some trees blossom in July and August; others in September and October. The striking flowers grow in large, prominent clusters.

On some trees, these masses are a showy orange, on others, coral; on still others, salmon-colored; and on many, a brilliant red. Oddly enough, there are more of these trees in California than in their native land, where it is rare and grows only in Western Australia.

The Red or Scarlet Flowering tree is the most beautiful of all the Eucalypts.

Its many flower clusters produce an abundance of fruit pods in early fall. These "bowls" are used for ornamental purposes.

Note that in addition to the wooden, bowl-shaped fruit pods, there are many buds on this tree.

The Flowering Eucalyptus leaf is very much like the Indian Fig Tree leaf, now a popular street tree in Southern California.

PINK MELALEUCA

Young as well as old Pink Melaleuca trees are commonly found in front of homes and in city parks. The Melaleucas are also called Bottlebrush.

In July, August, and September, the numerous fluffy pink or purplish pompons at the tips of twigs attract attention.

These flowers produce a small woody fruit, through which several new leafy stems grow, thus lengthening the twigs. Melaleuca fruit stays on the trees for years.

The leaves of this evergreen are very small—most of them only a half an inch long. They are pale green and grow all around the stem.

The bark is whitish. Even on young trees, the bark sheds.

The gnarled branches and slender trunks of older Melaleuca trees have fantastic horizontal lengths and crooked shapes.

BOTTLEBRUSH

The Bottlebrush is a favorite lawn or patio tree and is also seen on many boulevard islands.

It has drooping branches with brilliant, showy red flower clusters surrounding the stems. The dense cylindrical spikes, at the tips of each branch, resemble a bottlebrush.

The flowers are in full bloom, off and on, from May through November.

New leafy parts start where the flowers end. Later, new stems grow through the woody pods, since an eccentric gray woody fruit is created when the flowering stage is over. These woody pods are three to four inches in length and remain on the trees for years.

The leaves are gray-green and grow to three and a half inches long and three quarters of an inch wide. They are leathery in texture and turn reddish in March and April.

The trunk of the tree is narrow; the bark is light gray with raised, wart-like marks.

The Bottlebrush is an evergreen.

Another popular kind of Bottlebrush has leaves which are willow-like and slender, soft, and downy—only one and a half inches long and one quarter of an inch wide. This type is more apt to be a bush than a tree.

OLIVE

Another popular evergreen and ornamental tree is the Olive. It is medium-sized and usually has a gnarled trunk.

The branches, as well as the opposite twigs, point upward.

The dull, gray-green leaves are opposites, too. They are simple and smooth-margined. The slender, lance-shaped leaves are three inches long, half an inch wide, and leathery in texture.

The insignificant flowers of the Olive tree blossom in April and May. They are followed by purple olives—these look black against the silver of the leaves.

To be edible, the olives must first be processed.

The olive branch has always been a symbol of Peace.

In the Holy Land, on the Mount of Olives, there are said to be eight ancient Olive trees, dating from the time of Christ, still bearing fruit today.

ACACIA LONGIFOLIA

In Australia, this Acacia tree is known as the Sydney Golden Wattle. In the United States, there are a dozen or so varieties of Acacia.

The leaf of this *Acacia longifolia* is olive-green in color. It is three to six inches long and three quarters of an inch wide and has a tiny stalk.

These evergreen leaves alternate with spikes of bright golden-yellow flower clusters on long twigs. The clusters are elongated; they are made up of many florets.

In California, the blossoms appear from March through May. In warmer climates, some Acacias bloom twice a year.

This ornamental Acacia has a sweet, pleasant, perfume-like aroma when its cylindrical clusters of flowers are out. These clusters grow to over two inches.

Stringbean-like seedpods appear in May and June. When they mature, they split open and expose beady black seeds.

BLACKWOOD ACACIA

The Blackwood Acacia, a tall shade tree, can be seen on many city streets. The trunks are usually divided and the tree has many branches.

The bark is rough and the foliage plentiful. The slender leaves, more like blades of grass, are only two to three inches long. They are dark green, simple, flat and very narrow—only one quarter of an inch wide.

In spite of its being an evergreen, about the only time this tree calls attention to itself is in April. At that time, for a few days only, you can see a profuse mass of cream-colored, compact flower clusters, such as those in the photograph opposite.

The tree is especially lovely when the sun shines on these small balls of tiny flowers.

ACACIA

Of the hundreds of Acacias introduced from Australia, the best-known is this species, popularly called Mimosa. Botanically, this is incorrect, as *Mimosa* technically refers to a quite different group of plants.

In the spring, when this tree is in bloom, there is a delicious fragrance of perfume from the large clusters of flowers.

Each cluster of these golden-yellow flowers has an abundance of tiny round, fluffy balls. Each ball, only one quarter of an inch in size, grows singly on a tinier stem and is made up of thirty to forty of the tiniest florets.

The foliage, often hidden under the mass of yellow flowers, is equally abundant. The grayish-green leaves, about four to six inches long, are fernlike, finely divided and twice pinnately compound. That is, each pair of one to two inch feather-like leaflets again has thirty or more pairs of the tiniest one-quarter inch leaflets.

The plumy sprays seem evergreen but are really deciduous. Each year, a new yellow-green growth takes the place of the old leaves as they shed.

The leaflets fold up each night. The branchlets are slim and brittle.

The smooth thin bark has fine vertical markings. It peels in scales and exudes a cinnamon-reddish gum-like substance when punctured.

The fruit begins to appear in August. It is flat, twisted and stringbean-like, and splits open when ripe.

Being a subtropical importation, the Acacia, a popular garden and street tree, requires a warm climate.

SILK TREE

In the South, this ornamental patio tree is commonly called Mimosa. Both South and West, it is also known as the Powder Puff Tree. Botanists call it *Albizia*.

The Silk Tree is particularly attractive from late spring through late summer, when its small clusters of dainty, silk, pink puffs are in full bloom. The showy, fluffy ball-like flowers are two inches in diameter.

Some flowers are pale; some brilliant; all closely resemble pompons. They are soft, have no fragrance, and each lasts only a few days. However, other flowers bloom in close succession, so that the tree is in bloom and attractive all summer.

The branches of this small, subtropical wide-spreading tree grow in tiers. All along the Silk Tree branches, but especially at the tips, there are clusters of doubly-compound fern-like leaves.

These leaves have individual two-inch stalks. Each leaf is about ten inches long and about five inches across. Each has eight to fourteen pairs of compound leaflets. These finely divided leaflets, in turn, have about thirty to forty tiny one-half inch leaflets.

The handsome, feathery foliage is yellow-green and, like the Acacia, folds up at night. In November, the tree is entirely leafless; only a few seedpods may still be hanging on.

If you will look closely at the photograph below you will see several of these long, flat, stringbean-like seedpods.

The bark of the Silk Tree is dark gray and fairly smooth.

JACARANDA

The Jacaranda is an exciting tree even without its showy flowers. Its foliage is equally interesting because of its delicate, fernlike, and lacy appearance.

The light green terminal leaves are pinnately compound. They are about ten inches long and grow opposite each other in pairs, on two-inch leaf stalks.

Each leaf has sixteen or more compound leaflets, in pairs. Each of these, in turn, again has about twenty pairs of tiny leaflets.

In September, the ground under the tree is littered with wilted flowers. At the same time, flat round, hard, woody seedpods begin to dangle. They are about two inches in diameter and look like dance castanets.

Some leaves fall off in April. The tree, however, remains bare only until May.

The bark of the tree is light grayish-brown and smooth.

There is nothing more beautiful than a row of large, picturesque Jacaranda trees in bloom.

From May to September in California, crowds stop to admire this popular, aristocratic, patio, park, and street tree.

It has striking clusters of blue, lavender, violet or purplish flowers, in profusion, at the tips of twigs. Visitors from the east and abroad are often thrilled when they see the handsome Jacaranda flowers for the first time.

It is small wonder that some residents call the Jacaranda their favorite tree. It is charming, luxurious, and colorful. The loose, eye-catching clusters of flowers are about eight inches long. Each consists of numerous brilliant two-inch bell-shaped flowers. No photograph can ever do the Jacaranda justice!

SILK OAK

These ornamental trees like warm climate. You will find many on streets in southern California.

The Silk Oak is a tall, slender, attractive evergreen. It usually has two or more divided trunks high up and also many branches. All the branches curve upward. The gray-brown bark is rough and furrowed.

In late spring and early summer, the Silk Oak is very striking because of the numerous clusters of orange flowers. These have red spots and grow in graceful, decorative sprays in slender, tendril-like fashion.

These two photographs give you a closer look at the tendril-like flowers and a leaf of the Silk Oak.

When the flowers and fruit are gone, this subtropical tree is a solid mass of beautiful, decorative, lacy leaves.

The dark green fern-like foliage is distinctive. Each compound leaf is six to twelve inches long. The leaves are light green on top and silvery and silky underneath.

Each leaflet has two or more narrow pointed divisions. The leaves grow at the tip of each branch. Silk Oak leaves fade and hang on all winter. Some are tan, some gold, and some dark brown.

As new leaves come out in April, the dried leaves drop off. Whenever it rains, the leaves fall and create silhouettes on the sidewalks.

CHINESE ELM

This handsome, small, shade tree is planted on paths in parks, on sidewalks, as well as on many a front lawn, as in the photograph above.

The Chinese Elm is an evergreen. The tiny leaves are rose-colored when new. They turn green. When mature, they are a glossy dark green and are two and a half inches in length and one half inch in width.

The drooping branches are alternate and have as many as twenty of these simple, alternate, long-pointed leaves on each slender twig. When the weather gets cold, some of the leaves turn red and drop off.

If you will look closely at the photograph on this page, you will notice that the base of each leaf is lopsided, just like any large Elm leaf of the American or European species.

Chinese Elm trees blossom and fruit in the fall when the leaves fall. In October, the long stems are covered with light green winged nuts (three eighths of an inch long) that stand out among the few remaining dark green leaves.

If one did not expect this fruit to be on the tree, it would give the impression of a parasitic growth of numerous tiny bright green leaves.

The trunk of the Chinese Elm is narrow and its light tan bark is not as smooth as it seems. A close-up (on this page) reveals its mottled design of brown dots. A lighter inner bark shows through, where the outer bark has shed in spots.

Not all Chinese Elms are as small as this front lawn tree. On many a street and in parks, they are wider, and often as tall as fifty feet.

CORAL

This Coral is known as *Erythrina coralloides*. *Erythrina* means red. There are many kinds of Coral trees from tropical and subtropical America and Africa. This one is cultivated in southern California.

Since all are handsome and ornamental, one or another will be found on front lawns and for miles down the center of boulevards.

Its showy flowers (photograph opposite) burst forth early in May and blossom all through June. These clusters appear only at the tips of the branches.

The brilliant red flowers are all the more spectacular because the entire tree is leafless at first.

As the flowers drop off, the leaves come out gradually, one by one. Once all the flowers are gone, the tree is thickly covered with leaves for many months. There are small thorns on the twigs and leaf stems.

The leaf of this Coral (above) is made up of three heart-shaped leaflets. Each leaflet has a separate stalk; the two at the sides are only one half inch long, while the terminal leaflet stalk is two inches long. The leaf itself has a stalk six inches long.

In November, the leaves turn yellow. During the winter and spring, the branches are completely bare except for many large sharp thorns on the trunk of the tree.

COCKSPUR CORAL

The *Erythrina cristagallii* (photograph above) is popularly known as the Cockspur Coral.

Its leaves also are composed of three leaflets each, but they are narrow, not heart-shaped.

There are no thorns at all on the branches or on the trunk of the Cockspur Coral tree. Only the leaf stalks have tiny, sharp thorns.

The exotic-looking flower is even more striking than the Coral described previously. For one thing, it is two-toned—crimson and coral. Unlike the *Erythrina coralloides*, which has the flowers only at the tips of branches, the Cockspur Coral has many flowers along the branch. These flowers bloom a long time. Some appear in the summer, others in early fall, on the same tree.

From the photograph above, you will see that there is not a single leaf on those branches which are covered with flowers. At the same time the tree has many branches with only leaves.

In October, when the petals have folded, the flowers are even more distinctive. Each resembles a lobster claw!

CREPE MYRTLE

Because the blossoms grow in prominent masses and are long-lasting, and because leaves change color in the fall, the Crepe Myrtle tree attracts attention on lawns and boulevards in southern California a good part of the year.

Some of the trees have white flowers, others pink, still others lavender or purple. These grow in upright clusters at the tips of each twig. Each of the abundant clusters is four to eight inches tall.

The individual crinkled flower, only one and a half inches long, looks like crepe-paper, because each of its five to eight petals is ruffled and fringed. The flowers bloom from late June through to September.

I first saw this lovely little tree in Williamsburg, in the South.

The leaves are narrowly oval. They grow in pairs, directly from the main stem, without stalks.

The leaves are bright green when the flowers bloom. They turn red or gold in the autumn, before they fall off.

Green seed capsules form brown woody clusters which open partly and hang on.

The bark is smooth, light brown when young. Older trees, whose outer flaky bark has shed, show an inner pinkish bark as well as some dark patches.

ORANGE PITTOSPORUM

There are many species of Pittosporum. While most persons pronounce it "Pittospo′rum," scientists prefer "Pittos′porum."

However you say it, the Orange Pittosporum (*Pittosporum undulatum*) is an attractive and conspicuous tree at all seasons.

From January to July, you not only see the lovely small white, waxy flowers, but you smell them. They are as fragrant as orange blossoms; the tree is therefore sometimes called Mock Orange.

Each flower is on a separate half-inch stalk. There are as many as eight little flowers in each cluster. These produce clusters of green berries.

By November, the berries begin to turn a lovely orange—not unlike, but a bit larger and rounder than, the berries shown in the photograph on the opposite page. When mature, the berries split open, and the smooth red-brown seeds with their sticky covering are exposed.

The dark, glossy evergreen foliage is handsome, too. The wavy-edged leaves grow in clusters, at the tips of twigs on wide-spreading branches.

DIAMOND-LEAVED PITTOSPORUM

Another common street tree is this Diamond-leaved Pittosporum. It derives its name from the shape of its leaves, which grow in clusters at the tips of twigs.

Each leaf is broad in the middle and tapers to a point at top and bottom. Each leaf is irregularly toothed at its two upper sides but smooth at its two lower sides.

Early in the summer the tree bears large flat clusters of cream-white flowers—not unlike those in the photograph on the opposite page.

By December, the flowers produce clusters of lovely orange-colored berries—such as shown in the photograph above. The tree is conspicuous because of these berries, which stand out among the rich, dark green foliage.

When the berries of the Diamond-leaved Pittosporum split open, they reveal small bead-like sticky black seeds. The name "Pittosporum" means sticky seed.

67

WILLOW PITTOSPORUM

The name "Pittosporum" is given numerous trees of vastly different appearance, which are, however, related. This tree is a Willow Pittosporum. Its leaf is very different from the Orange Pittosporum.

This small tree, originally imported from Australia, resembles a Weeping Willow, because of its many slender, drooping branches and branchlets.

There are many narrow leaf-blades on each of these branchlets. The Willow Pittosporum leaves grow to three inches long, or longer, but are only one quarter inch wide. They are light green. Each has its own one quarter inch stalk.

The small flowers are yellow and grow singly.

By August, colorful orange berries begin to appear and soon split open.

The bark of the Willow Pittosporum is so light and smooth that it tempts vandals to carve their initials on it.

PODOCARPUS

The name *Podocarpus* comes from the Greek: *podos* meaning foot and *karpos* meaning fruit. Another name for Podocarpus is Plum Yew.

The flowers resemble the acacia—small, round, yellow flowers in clusters.

The tree is slender and erect. Its branches go upward but its branchlets hang. It is an evergreen.

Each of its thin twigs has as many as fifteen soft, bright green, slender, willow-like leaves. These flat leaves do not have separate stalks.

On some twigs, the leaves are alternate; on others, opposite each other. Both groups may be on the same branch.

While I have for years bought the coarser florist-shop variety of Podocarpus for flower arrangements in the east and have seen several species of Podocarpus in the west, I have yet to see any of the plum-like fleshy fruit the experts speak of. This is perhaps explained by the fact that the male and female Podocarpus are separate trees. The ones I pass daily may all be male!

PEPPER TREE

In southern California, the Pepper Tree is a common yet distinctive lawn and street tree. It is a subtropical evergreen.

Its low, gracefully drooping branches give one an opportunity to observe easily the handsome lacy foliage and the tiny flowers.

In August and September you will see clusters of the tiny five-petalled white flowers at the tips of twigs. As small as they are, you will notice that they have a yellow pin-dot center.

The foliage is olive-green. The compound, narrow leaves are twelve inches long. Each leaf has as many as thirty pointed leaflets.

When you crush a leaf or stem, you detect a peppery odor.

The picturesque Pepper Tree is especially attractive in the winter when the coral-red berries are out in long, showy, drooping clusters. Each berry is only one quarter inch in diameter.

From a distance, the Pepper Tree looks like a willow, but as you drive or walk by it you soon see the difference—especially when the tree has the hanging bunches of bright, red, beadlike berries.

If the handsome Pepper Tree you see all year around never has any of these berries, it is probably a male tree.

The bark of older trees is rough and shaggy.

BRAZILIAN PEPPER TREE

This lovely evergreen is fast becoming as popular as the better-known California Pepper Tree.

More and more you see it on front lawns, as well as in newly planted rows on city streets.

The flower of the Brazilian Pepper Tree is small and white.

At Christmas time, the tree attracts considerable attention because of its bright, red berries. Each berry is only one eighth inch in diameter and has a separate tiny stalk.

The berries grow in short thick clusters—some are flat, some upright, and some hang.

The leaves of the Brazilian Pepper Tree are only six to eight inches long. Each leaf has seven small, broad leaflets. These are thick; they are dark green above and paler underneath.

The bark of the tree is rough.

CAROB

The sturdy branches of the Carob have numerous twigs, each of which has several compound leaves. They seem to grow layer upon layer and create a beautiful design.

Each shiny dark green leaf has six to ten broad, oval two-inch leaflets, in pairs.

Under the oddly contorted branches of a female tree, you will see many chocolate-brown seedpods hanging in groups.

The inside pulp of this fruit, which is known as St. John's Bread, is sweet. It is edible in the autumn when it is ripe.

The Carob is a handsome, ornamental, evergreen shade tree. Rows of them can be seen on many city sidewalks.

Seen from underneath its spreading branches, the tree looks as if it had a dome top. You do not even have to be a tree-enthusiast to notice the exquisite pattern the leafy branches of a Carob tree make.

While male trees do not bear fruit, in October you can see inconspicuous flowers sprouting out directly from the branches. Later on, "knobs" appear where the flowers were.

We were fortunate to find a tree with an unusual number of bare branches, so we could show you how these knobs look. Actually, these "warts" are the stubs of branchlets on which the male flowers had grown.

CAMPHOR TREE

This popular ornamental evergreen was originally imported from China and Japan. Many long streets are lined on both sides with these Camphor shade trees.

The Camphor Tree is attractive at all seasons. In the early spring, the shiny, light green leaves turn crimson, then drop off. By May, new bright chartreuse-colored leaves appear, along with clusters of inconspicuous yellow flowers.

The new leaves have a delicate pinkish tip which catches the eye. Even from blocks away, you simply cannot miss the "halo" effect on the round tops of these trees.

The leaves are alternate. They grow to five inches long and are two inches wide. Each has an individual stalk of one to two inches.

In the winter, small black berries stand out against the glossy green leaves. At any season, when you crush a leaf, you get a distinct, medicinal, aromatic camphor fragrance. The entire tree has an aroma.

The bark of the Camphor Tree is rough; many widespreading branches stem from a single trunk, as you can see from the photograph on the opposite page.

Look closely at the photograph above and you will notice two "dots" on the smallest leaf, near the stem. These are camphor glands. They show on both the upper and under sides of each leaf.

SOUTHERN MAGNOLIA

The Southern Magnolia, or *Magnolia grandiflora*, is a handsome, ornamental, street tree.

The large, showy, white flowers are cup-shaped, waxlike and fragrant. Some flowers are as much as ten inches across.

80

Along with a number of fully opened blossoms, there can be many buds at the same time.

Although this photograph was taken in August, the tree already has some fruit on its branches, as you can see.

The fruit is erect, cone-shaped and soft—about four inches long. In October, bright red seeds in these cones attract birds as well as passers-by.

On the Pacific Coast, this evergreen blossoms often. Whether it is May or November or any other time of the year, you can always see at least a flower or two on some Magnolia tree.

The leathery leaves of the Southern Magnolia are five to eight inches long. They are handsome, glossy green above and cocoa-brown underneath. The edges of the leaves are smooth. Each leaf has its own inch-long stalk.

The wide-spreading branches of the tree are heavily weighted with leaves all year round. As some of the leaves drop off, new ones come out. Toward the end of September, the leaves are most notice-able, because they begin to curl up and show more of the lovely brown of the underside than the shiny green side.

A tree which can easily be mistaken for the Magnolia is the Moreton Bay Fig Tree, or Ficus. You can tell the Moreton by its multiple trunk. On some trees, the leathery, brown-backed leaves of the Moreton are smaller than those of the Magnolia. Then again, on others, they may be as large as the leaves of a Rubber Tree.

Today the Indian Fig has become a popular street tree. The light bark of the Indian Fig is very much like the Moreton Bay Fig. The Indian Fig leaf is much smaller and is green on both sides.

In the southeast, this Southern Magnolia is so popular that both Louisiana and Mississippi have it as their State Tree.

There are three true cedars—

THE ATLAS CEDAR

THE CEDAR OF LEBANON, and

THE DEODAR.

Of these, the handsome, ornamental Atlas Cedar, especially the glauca variety with its distinctive blue-green foliage, is the easiest to recognize.

ATLAS CEDAR

The needle-leaves of the Atlas Cedar are the shortest of the three true cedars—not over an inch long.

Notice, in the photograph facing this page, that the tightly compact rosette clusters all have practically the same sized needle-leaves. These leaves grow out of tiny spurs and are crowded very closely together.

New stubby needles grow singly all around the tips of stems and are skimpy at the ends.

The cones are small and ooze resin.

Most important: the horizontal branches of the Atlas Cedar are the stiffest of the three true cedars.

It takes an expert to differentiate the other two cedars. These hints may help:

While the Atlas Cedar has the shortest needle (one inch), and the Deodar the longest (two inches), the Cedar of Lebanon has a one-and-a-half inch needle-leaf.

The Cedar of Lebanon needles form flat rosette clusters. While they are also out of tiny spurs, they are not as close together as the Atlas Cedar.

The Deodar needles do not have spurs. They grow directly out of the stems. Instead of compact rosettes, the Deodar needles form loose bundles and are not too close together.

Finally, the top of a Cedar of Lebanon is apt to be flat, whereas the tip of a Deodar is usually a graceful curve.

In the Biblical days of King Solomon, Cedars were abundant in Lebanon forests. Today, only a few Cedar trees can be seen there.

DEODAR

This beautiful, symmetrical evergreen tree was introduced from India. In California, you see avenue after avenue lined with Deodar trees.

The most distinctive feature of a Deodar is that its uppermost branch, silhouetted against the sky, reaches up, then tips over in a graceful curve, as if it were nodding.

The wide-spreading branches of the Deodar are very flexible and curve downward, the lowest almost or actually touching the ground.

In late July, new bright green needle-leaves appear singly all around, at the tips of the drooping stems.

Being pyramidal in shape, Deodars are often trimmed outdoors with colored electric lights at Christmas time.

The Deodar is identified by its foliage as well as its tip. The two-inch needle-leaves are the longest of the three true cedars.

Without any spurs, these needles grow in clustered bundles on each side of the stem. Each bundle contains needles both two inches and one inch long.

Because there are fewer bundles and these are not too close together, the Deodar foliage does not form as compact a rosette as the Atlas Cedar.

The cones of the Deodar are originally light green. The male cones remain small. They turn brown and burst apart right on the branches.

The female cones grow to four inches long and one and a half inches wide.

JUNIPER

This small ornamental Chinese Juniper, an evergreen, is related to the Cypress. The European Cypress trees are tall and slender and look like exclamation points in a landscape—such as one sees especially in Italy.

The leaves of the Juniper are bright green. There are two kinds of needle-leaves on the same shoot: short, sharp awl-shaped needles, in whorls of three, going out at angles, and flat overlapping scales that hug the twigs.

Even the woody branches are so scale-covered that they are almost invisible. Each curved twig is thickly covered with overlapping flat, short, scale-like needle-leaves. These are closely pressed, circling the tiny stems. The stems, in turn, hug the twigs which twist upward around the curved branches.

The Juniper has a tiny bluish-gray, waxy, berry-like fruit. It is only one third of an inch in diameter and contains the seeds. Only the female trees have these berries.

This particular Juniper tree, as you will see from the photograph on the opposite page, has a second trunk at its base.

At Yosemite, there are hardy Juniper trees of another species, said to be 2,500 years old.

REDWOOD

The Redwood is an aromatic tree with long, graceful, drooping branches and an attractive, thick, reddish-brown fibrous bark. It is pyramidal in shape.

It has flat, needle-leaves which range from one third inch to one inch long, spread out on both sides of each branchlet.

New leaves are bright yellow-green; older ones, dark green. Often, dull brown leaves cling to the stems, even when dead.

The tiny pine cones grow at the tips of the branches.

Redwoods thrive best in areas where there is fog. At county shows, when they have Redwood displays, they create an artificial atmosphere of fog, to keep the trees alive.

Several groves of Redwoods, the tallest living trees in the world, are protected in forests along the Pacific Coast, by the United States Government as well as by the State of California.

The Redwood, a native, is the California State Tree.

CRYPTOMERIA

In Japan recently, I saw the stately Cryptomeria everywhere.

It is a tall, slender, spire-like evergreen. In California it is used as an ornamental street and garden tree. Landscape architects call the Cryptomeria an "accent" tree in their designs.

Its tiny, awl-shaped, needle-like leaves—only one quarter to one half inch long—are curved and sharply pointed. These leaves cover the twigs thickly and closely. As with most conifers, young leaves are different from older ones.

Before they drop off, some Cryptomeria leaves turn a lovely cocoa-brown in August. At the same time, bright new green leaves, growing out at the tips of the branchlets, accentuate the older, dark green leaves.

Botanically, the Cryptomeria is related to the *Sequoia gigantea*. Small prickly cones also grow at the tips of the branchlets.

The bark of the Cryptomeria is dark brown. It has a reddish inner bark which shows through in spots.

Another variety of Cryptomeria has softer, almost feathery needles. These turn a bronze color before they fall.

STAR PINE

This distinctive, pyramidal tree is also known as Norfolk Island Pine and *Araucaria excelsa.*

Because its stiff branches are so symmetrical and its foliage so different from any other tree, the formal Star Pine attracts attention. In spite of its name, the bright green twisted foliage is unlike any real Pine.

The narrow trunk—which grows straight up—is encircled from the very ground to the top, with five to seven thick branches emanating at the same level, at evenly spaced intervals.

These beautifully proportioned branches arrange themselves, like spokes of a wheel, forming regular whorls all the way up.

The higher up each group, the shorter the branches become. At the very tip of the tree, the uppermost whorl, being the smallest, forms a star.

From the bottom up, each ropelike branch spreads out horizontally. Each is bare near the trunk but full of cylindrical branchlets, in pairs, at the tips. Here again, each branchlet becomes shorter and shorter until at the tip of the branch it is a mere point.

Each tiny leaf is needle-like and awl-shaped, sharp-pointed and curved. The leaves overlap in a linked fashion. This gives the branchlet its cylindrical shape. In September, when some crisp, tan, dried branchlets fall to the ground, they look and feel like toy whips.

When the Star Pine is twenty or twenty-five years old, it has a very ragged appearance here in California. All too many of its branches are bare and the tree looks most unkempt. Oddly enough, in Japan or Honolulu, I never saw a Star Pine that was not in seemingly perfect condition. In Hawaii, they call the tree Araucaria and Christmas Tree.

JEFFREY PINE

Every one knows a Pine at sight because of the long, green needle-leaves. This giant mountain evergreen, the Jeffrey Pine, so closely resembles the Ponderosa Pine that some specialists consider it a variety of the Ponderosa.

The rugged Jeffrey thrives at 8,500-foot elevations in the California Sierra Nevada and in the Canadian Rockies. It is a straight tree. The twigs are purple when young.

Large clusters of slim eight-inch-long needles grow at the tips of each gracefully curved branchlet of the Jeffrey. The soft, flexible needles are yellow-green when young and dark blue-green at maturity. The crushed needles smell like citrus fruit.

Jeffrey Pine needles grow in groups of three and are bound in a tan paper-like sheath at the base. The three needles are so shaped that they can be fitted together to form one thick needle.

The bark of the Jeffrey Pine is a lovely red-brown color. It has a distinct vanilla odor. Its smell is one good way to tell it from the Ponderosa Pine.

The cones are five to eight inches long. Some are light brown, and some are purple. All have tightly closed scales.

The scales of a Jeffrey Pine cone have inward-pointed prickles. This is one of its distinguishing characteristics.

PONDEROSA

This large forest tree, sometimes called Western Yellow Pine, also grows at 8,500 foot elevations.

Young Ponderosa Pine trees have a straight, cylindrical trunk with a yellow-brown bark. Older tree barks are cinnamon-red and flake off in odd shapes, leaving a scaly surface, fissured into ridges or large plates.

The cones are three to five inches long, turning from green to dark purple at maturity. Its scales are thick and prickly. The scales open outward. This helps to differentiate the Ponderosa from the Jeffrey.

The needles of the Ponderosa are stout, without pointed tips. They are dark, yellowish-green, and ten inches long. They are bound in bundles of three.

The Ponderosa Pine is a very tall thin tree, not as pyramidal as most Pines.

96

The loose spreading branches have heavy clusters of coarse tufty foliage at the ends. The twigs are orange-colored and even have a strong smell of orange.

As with all Pines, each of the three-needled groups is enclosed in a paper-like sheath at the base. If you put the three needles together, they also fit snugly to form one thick needle.

The Ponderosa Pine is Montana's State Tree.

REDWOODS *(Sequoia sempervirens)*

The famous Redwoods, *Sequoia sempervirens*, are the tallest living trees in the world. The tree was named in honor of Sequoyah, a Cherokee Indian Chief; *sempervirens* means evergreen.

These Redwoods have graceful spreading branches which droop. The branchlets have single, dark green, flat, needle-like leaves in pairs.

The barks of these Redwoods are a dark cinnamon-red. They are deeply fluted, widely furrowed, and about a foot thick.

Most of the Redwoods are over 300 feet tall. In spite of their height, they are only about twenty feet in diameter. The taller the tree, the farther from the ground will be its first branch—at least fifty feet up the trunk.

Considering that these handsome evergreens are the tallest living trees in the world, and that they grow from seed, it is amazing that the cones, which contain the seeds, are as tiny as one inch!

Being a native, the Redwood is California's State Tree.

You see many thousands of these giant trees as you drive along highways in northern California or go across from San Francisco to Muir Woods.

Whole forests of Redwoods are protected in several National Parks in California by the United States Government as well as in state parks by the State of California.

Until 1956, the "Founder's Tree" in Humboldt State Park, California, was considered the tallest known tree. Having lost its top, by lightning probably, it now measures only 346 feet instead of 364.

Today, the tallest living Redwood is the "New Tree" at Upper Bull Creek, California. It measures 360 feet high.

These Redwoods are 2,200 years old!

THE BIG TREES *(Sequoia gigantea)*

Until recently, the California Big Trees, *Sequoia gigantea*, were always considered not only the largest living trees but the oldest. In 1957, however, some dwarf Pines were found which have outlived the pyramidal giants by almost a thousand years.

This still leaves the magnificent *Sequoia gigantea*, our California Big Trees, the largest living trees in the world.

Thousands of these massive trees can be seen in forests preserved by the United States Government in Sequoia National Park, in the Sierra Nevada Mountains, and also at Mariposa Grove in Yosemite National Park.

Big Trees prefer high altitudes and thrive even at an 8,500 foot elevation. In winter in the Sierra, in spite of thirty-foot snowdrifts, most of the ruddy trunks show—since the lowest bough may be all of 130 feet up.

These trees are truly so big that the branches alone are often seven feet in diameter and extend seventy feet out.

The light, cinnamon-red barks of the *Sequoia gigantea* are up to two feet thick. They are fibrous, and are widely as well as deeply furrowed.

The dark brown cones of the *Sequoia gigantea* are three inches high, egg-shaped, and woody.

Big Trees have dense masses of blue-green, scale-like, sharp-pointed foliage which overlaps and hugs the branchlets spirally.

The very largest of the Big Trees, the "General Sherman" in Sequoia National Park (although it has not been measured by ring count) is estimated to be 3,500 years old. Its huge trunk, over 272 feet tall, has a diameter of 34 feet and a base circumference of 101 feet.

BRISTLECONE PINE *(Pinus aristata)*

In 1957, the late Dr. Edmund Schulman, Professor of Tree-ring Research of the University of Arizona, Tucson, discovered several ancient live Bristlecone Pines.

When he measured some of these trees, with his "increment bore" instrument, he found three of them to be 4,500 years old. One greatly distorted tree, according to his ring-count has survived more than 4,600 years!

These gnarled trees are living driftwood on cliffs, high up in the White Mountains of Inyo National Forest. This is a dry region in the east-central part of California.

The ancient Bristlecone dwarfs are short—only ten to thirty feet tall. Their trunks are thick. The top limbs are smooth, irregular, and upright. The lower ones droop.

The bark is dull, light brown, shallowly furrowed.

The foliage is densely clustered at the ends of twigs. The short, deep green needle-leaves are one and a half inches long. There are five needles in each cluster. These are covered with tiny specks of pitch.

The cones are large, their scales tipped with long bristles which prick. The brown cones have a purplish tinge.

For every year of its life, each tree—except for the Palm—will add a layer of wood or growth ring. Changes in weather affect the growth of trees and show up in these rings. In wet years, the layers are large. In years of drought, the rings are small.

By counting the layers or rings of growth, experts can tell the age of a tree. Since the Bristlecone Pines exist only in a very dry area, their rings are naturally much closer together than those of any other tree.

Some day someone may find an older tree, but this much is certain: the oldest living thing in the world is a tree.

CULTIVATED TREES IN THE WEST
FROM THESE FAR-AWAY PLACES

AFRICA
  Atlas Cedar (North Africa)
  Coral (South Africa)
  Podocarpus

ASIA
  Crepe Myrtle (South Asia)
  Silk Tree

AUSTRALIA
  Acacia
  Bottlebrush
  Diamond-leaved
    Pittosporum
  Eucalyptus
  King Palm
  Orange Pittosporum
  Pink Melaleuca
  Silk Oak
  Star Pine
  Willow Pittosporum

BRAZIL
  Coral
  Jacaranda
  Pepper Tree
  Plume or Queen Palm

CANARY ISLANDS (off north-
west Africa, in Atlantic)
  Date Palm

CHINA
  Camphor Tree
  Chinese Elm
  Crepe Myrtle

Juniper
Windmill Palm

EUROPE (Mediterranean
Region)
  Carob
  Italian Cypress
  Olive

INDIA
  Crepe Myrtle
  Deodar Cedar

JAPAN
  Camphor Tree
  Cryptomeria

MEXICO
  Acacia
  Coral
  Fan Palm
  Yucca

NEW ZEALAND
  Pittosporum

PERSIA
  Silk Tree

PERU
  Pepper Tree

PORTUGAL
  Coral

WEST INDIES
  Podocarpus
  Yucca

EASTERN TREES IN THE WEST

To avoid duplication, the thirty-one trees below (from *A First Book of Tree Identification*) are omitted here, although all are seen somewhere in the West.

Ailanthus
Arbor Vitae Cedar
Aspen
Ash

Beech
Bitternut Hickory
Black Locust
Blue Spruce

Catalpa

Dogwood

Gingko
Golden Larch
Gray Birch

Hackberry
Hemlock
Holly
Horse Chestnut

Linden

Magnolia

Norway Maple

Paulownia
Pin Oak
Pine
Plane Tree

Red Oak

Sassafras
Slippery Elm
Sweetgum

Tulip Tree

Weeping Willow
Wild Black Cherry

In the book these are arranged by "look alikes." Before the book was published, I found all but one of these trees in Griffith Park in Los Angeles, twenty-eight of them in Golden Gate Park in San Francisco, and twenty-nine in Cheesman and City Parks in Denver, Colorado.

Also most of the thirty-one trees can be seen in various parts of Canada. Then again, in 1960, on my trip around the world, I was pleasantly surprised to find almost all of them in practically every country, especially where there is plenty of rain.

Many years ago, I was amazed to read, in several tree books, that the "Paulownia does not grow north of Philadelphia." Even then I knew where there was a lovely Paulownia tree right in Central Park, New York. Also I recalled having one pointed out to me near a children's camp way up in Maine years earlier.

With the way trees, like people, are transplanted—climate permitting—no one can say that this or that tree is not found here or there.

STATE TREES

Alabama—Slash Pine
Alaska—Sitka Spruce
Arizona—Mesquite
Arkansas—Shortleaf Pine

California—Redwood
Colorado—Blue Spruce
Connecticut—White Oak

Delaware—American Holly

Florida—Palmetto

Georgia—Live Oak

Hawaii—Kukui—better known as the Candlenut

Idaho—Western White Pine
Illinois—Bur Oak
Indiana—Tulip Tree
Iowa—Black Walnut

Kansas—Cottonwood
Kentucky—Tulip Tree

Louisiana—Southern Magnolia

Maine—White Pine
Maryland—White Oak
Massachusetts—American Elm
Michigan—Apple
Minnesota—Eastern White Pine
Mississippi—Southern Magnolia
Missouri—English Hawthorn
Montana—Ponderosa Pine

Nebraska—American Elm
Nevada—One-leaf Pinyon
New Hampshire—White Birch
New Jersey—Red Oak
New Mexico—Pinyon Pine
New York—Sugar Maple
North Carolina—Flowering Dogwood
North Dakota—American Elm

Ohio—Buckeye
Oklahoma—Redbud, Judas Tree
Oregon—Douglas Fir

Pennsylvania—Hemlock

Rhode Island—Maple

South Carolina—Palmetto
South Dakota—Black Hills Spruce

Tennessee—Tulip Poplar
Texas—Pecan

Utah—Blue Spruce

Vermont—Sugar Maple
Virginia—Flowering Dogwood

Washington—Western Hemlock
West Virginia—Sugar Maple
Wisconsin—Sugar Maple
Wyoming—Cottonwood

PINK MELALEUCA
see page 43

ACACIA LONGIFOLIA
see page 49

BOTTLEBRUSH
see page 45

ACACIA (MIMOSA)
see page 53

SILK TREE
see page 54

JACARANDA
see page 57

SILK OAK
see page 58

CORAL
see page 63

COCKSPUR CORAL
see page 63

DIAMOND-LEAVED PITTOSPORUM
see page 67

CREPE MYRTLE
see page 64

BRAZILIAN PEPPER TREE
see page 74

'EPPER TREE
ee page 73

RED FLOWERING EUCALYPTUS
see page 40

JERUSALEM THORN

A native of Arizona, the Jerusalem Thorn is planted as a park and street tree in desert towns of Southern California.

Early in the spring, this small tree attracts attention. Its zig-zagging branches have odd, long, slim, spiny, yellowish-green branchlets with forty to eighty tiny (one-eighth inch) light green leaflets, in pairs.

Masses of showy star-like, bright yellow flowers appear early in the summer. In the fall, the tree has dark, drooping fruit-pods resembling string beans.

TECHNICAL TERMS EXPLAINED

These do not all appear in my text but since they are used frequently, in books and magazine articles, tree enthusiasts might like to know them.

alternate—leaves, twigs, or branches staggered singly but never opposite each other.
arboretum—a place where trees and shrubs are cultivated and hybrids developed through experiments. It is often called a botanical garden.
asymmetrical—uneven; lopsided.
awl-shaped—a narrow needle-leaf tapering to a point.

bark—the outer covering of a trunk or branch.
bipinnate—doubly compound; each leaflet pinnate (like the Acacia).
branch—a subdivision of a main stem.
bract—sheath from the axil of which the flower or stem arises.
bristle-tipped—a leaf or cone with points ending with a stiff hair.

capsule—a dry fruit.
catkin—a furry cluster of inconspicuous flowers.
cluster—a group of two or more parts: flowers, fruit, etc.
compound—a leaf divided into a number of separate leaflets on the same stalk.
conifer—a needle or scaly-leaved tree bearing cones or a berry-like fruit.
conservatory—a glass greenhouse for growing and displaying plants.
crown—top of a tree.

deciduous—trees that are bare of leaves in fall or winter.
doubly compound—a leaf with leaflets which in turn have separate leaflets; same as bipinnate.
downy—covered with soft fine hairs.

elliptical—oval or oblong rounded leaves.
entire—leaves without lobes, division, or teeth.
evergreen—trees that have leaves all year round. All trees lose their leaves but not all at the same time since new leaves replace the old.

frond—a leaf, especially of a palm; also fern leaves.
fruit—the part containing seeds.

genus—a family group of trees (one or more species). Given first in a two-part scientific name and always spelled with a Capital letter.

hybrid—offspring of the union of a male of one species and the female of another.

indigenous—native to a region.
inflorescence—arrangement of flowers on a stem.

leaflet—a part of a compound leaf.
lobed—leaf divided with deep spaces (like Sycamore).

margin—the outside edge of a leaf.
midrib—central main vein of a leaf or leaflet.

needles—leaves shaped like a needle (Pine).

opposite—two leaves, twigs, or branches at the same level, opposite each other.

panicle—a compound flower cluster.
parasite—a plant living on another living organism at whose expense it obtains food.
pendulous—hanging.
perfect—bisexual flower having both male and female elements.
petiole—a leaf stalk.
pinnate—a compound leaf with leaflets on both sides of a stalk (like Pepper Tree). Also feather-like leaf with a main vein (like Canary Date Palm).
pinnately compound—same as doubly compound; a leaf with leaflets on both sides of a center vein—with these leaflets again having separate leaflets (Acacia).
pistil or pistillate—central female part of a flower in which the seeds will be formed.
pollen—the fine yellow fertilizing dust of a male flower.
pod—the part that contains the seeds; a fruit which usually splits at maturity.

serrate—notched or saw-toothed edge of a leaf.
scale—tiny leaves, as on a Cedar tree. Buds and cones also have scales.
scaly—like flakes on outer barks of trees.
sessile—without a stalk.

sheath—outside covering from beneath which a new branch may arise.
shrub—bushy woody growth—less than fifteen feet high.
simple leaf—a single leaf without subdivisions.
sinus—space between two lobes of a leaf.
spathe—large sheathing bract enclosing an inflorescence.
species—a number of plants of the same kind; possessing common characteristics. In scientific nomenclature, the designation of the species (the "specific" designation) always follows the genus name and is not capitalized.
spiny—a sharp point on a leaf, stem, twig, or branch.
stalk—any supporting structure.
stamen or staminate—the male pollen-bearing part of a flower.
stand—a number of trees on a given area.
stem—any axis which has leaves, flowers, or branches attached to it.

thorny—twigs with stiff woody sharp-pointed projections.
toothed—small sharp-pointed edges of a leaf.
true—the Latin name as originally recorded.
twice pinnately compound—a leaf with leaflets which again have separate leaflets (like the Acacia).

varieties—a group of related plants too trivial to be called a species.

whorl—arrangement of three or more leaflets, leaves, or twigs radiating in a circle from the same level around a stem or branch, or branches around a tree (as Star Pine).

Almost every tree has one or more common names but only one scientific or Latin (real) name. Scientists prefer to use these Latin names.

Each scientific name has two parts:
(a) The first or *Genus* which represents a group within a family. The *Genus* is always written with a capital letter.
(b) The second name, which follows the *Genus*, designates the *species* and represents all of the plants of the same kind including varieties. It is written with a small letter.

When a tree is spoken of as
small—it is up to thirty feet tall
medium—it is up to seventy feet, and
large—it is over seventy feet high.

INDEX

It is gratifying to know that schools be-gin tree identification and conservation projects for boys and girls as early as the fifth grade.

Also that CAMP FIRE GIRLS, GIRL *and* BOY SCOUTS, *and many other youth and adult groups adopt identification and tree programs as hobbies these days.*